An opinionated guide to

# VEGAN
# LONDON

T0124544

*Text by*
SARA KIYO POPOWA

*Photography by*
SAM A. HARRIS

# INFORMATION IS DEAD.
# LONG LIVE OPINION.

Why buy a guide book? Surely, everything to know is available online. True. But if you are like us, you don't want endless information, you want well-informed opinion.

With the expert insight of Sara Kiyo Popowa and original photography from Sam A. Harris, this book is a short guide to the best vegan hot-spots in town, from fast-food eateries to ultra-refined restaurants. It is unashamedly geared to both seasoned vegans and those more tentative. It is not our job to tell you why veganism is morally vital, but it is ours to celebrate that it's tasty, stylish and accessible to a much wider audience than many believe.

This is the reason we cover both the established destinations as well as the newer or more cutting edge, both of which would do a fine job of persuading the most hardened meat eater to consider a more plant-based diet. Veganism is mainstream, and nowhere more so than in London. Hooray to that.

*Ann and Martin*
Founders, Hoxton Mini Press

# CONTRIBUTORS

*Sara Kiyo Popowa* is a north London-based artist, recipe developer and photographer. Known as Shiso Delicious on Instagram, she is a keen advocate of plant-based food and a low-waste lifestyle and holds workshops and events in London and beyond. Sara is also the author of *Bento Power: Brilliantly Balanced Lunchbox Recipes*, which is inspired by her Swedish and Japanese heritage.

*shisodelicious.com  @shisodelicious*

*Sam A. Harris* is a travel and food photographer who lives in east London. He regularly shoots for *The Telegraph* and other publications, as well as directly with restaurants and chefs. Although most of the vegan food Sam tried was cold by the time he ate it, it still tasted pretty damn good.

*samaharris.com  @samaharris*

# INTRODUCTION

Vegan London is happening, and it's happening big. A new independent vegan place to eat seems to open every other week in this dynamic city, while familiar chain restaurants, fast-food joints and even the more high-end places are trying out vegan menus to feed the demand. Chefs are jumping at the challenge of creating new dishes, and with the number of vegans and vegan businesses on the rise, innovation and growth is at an all-time high. It's never been more exciting to be, or eat, vegan.

And who wouldn't be amazed by Club Mexicana's perfectly fishy tacos (no.37) which don't deplete any seas, or the creamy, artisan cheeses made entirely from plants at La Fauxmagerie's (no.15), or a perfectly seared abalone mushroom at Cub (no.20), given just as much skill and attention as any premium cut of meat?

This is 'food to win over meat eaters', to quote my omnivore friend who said this while we shared a tasty meal at Chinese hole-in-the-wall restaurant Mao Chow (no.29). Or, as Grace Regan, founder of curry house Spicebox (no.35) put it when I asked why she'd chosen not to make 'vegan' a big deal in her menu descriptions: 'Delicious, recognisable food is a way of getting people through the door. Once they taste how incredible vegan food can be, they change their mind about eating vegan.' This sums up a new, welcoming and all-encompassing vegan stance, one that proudly supports the fact that vegan food is just 'good food' that happens to be far better for the animals, human health (if done right) and the planet we live on. Whether or not to use the term 'vegan' is then down to personal choice.

So, what has brought this vegan wave here, powerful enough for London to be known as one of the most vegan-friendly cities on earth? It could be because British cuisine itself is a bit of a blank canvas and has already received plenty of influence from other cuisines (so adding one more to the mix isn't hard). London is also at a scale to support a multitude of creative, open-minded and experimental entrepreneurs – some of whose passionate work has pushed veganism into the mainstream. Social media plays a big role too, both in reach, and support, of vegan businesses. Many places in this book owe their speedy success to their online savviness and loyal following. Whatever the cause, the vegan scene is thriving in London – and we should all be thankful, not just the animals.

While researching (eating) and writing this book I noticed that east London is, so far, where the majority of vegan and vegan-friendly places are found. East being London's creative hub, made up from individuals with experimental values of life, could be a reason why. As vegan food gains momentum, I'd like to think we will see a more even distribution all over London (and the rest of the country, and world, too, I hope).

What you'll find here is not an exhaustive list, but a tightly curated selection of places I love and am happy to recommend; a mix of old and new-found gems I will go back to again and again. I hope you will enjoy this vegan guide to London as much as I enjoyed creating it together with brilliant photographer Sam A. Harris and the team at Hoxton Mini Press.

Go explore, try something you've never tasted before at the many inspiring places in this book – or eat something you've missed for years and you can now find a vegan version of. The vibrant, happening vegan scene is here to enjoy – and the more we support it and the talented, hard-working individuals behind it, the more we will see. The animals, your culinary sense of fun and many future generations will thank you for it.

*Sara Kiyo Popowa*
London, 2019

# THE BEST PLACES FOR...

### Brunch

Kick off the day at I Will Kill Again (East, no.14) with coffee and a slap-up savoury brunch. Or try Lele's (East, no.12) for drool-worthy comfort food like the stack of pillowy pancakes or scrambled tofu on sourdough.

### A date

Stoke your romantic glow at Kin + Deum (South, no.41) with aromatic Thai curries and tasty small plates. Or head to Genesis' cosmically decked-out diner (East, no.7) and tuck in to photogenic burgers and luminous cocktails.

### Special occasions

Serving the best of British plant produce, Cub (East, no.20) is the place to go for an eco-conscious fine dining experience. Farmacy's (West, no.42) nourishing salads and bowls, with superfood cocktails to match, will also hit the spot.

### Family gatherings

The Gate (West, no.44) is great for the whole family – wild mushroom risotto cake for grandpa and filled courgette flowers and polenta chips for the little nieces. Nem Nem's (North, no.47) Vietnamese menu is full of crowd-pleasing dishes, from crispy spring rolls to pho noodle soup.

### A junk food fix

Go for the mouth-watering Reuben sandwich and a generous portion of perfect fries at Rudy's Dirty Vegan Diner (North, no.46). Or try the ultra-crispy jackfruit wings and satisfying burgers at Biff's Jack Shack (East, no.8).

### Catching up with friends

The Spread Eagle (East, no.37) has it all – great booze, delicious food by Club Mexicana and ace ambience. For a vegan mozzarella-fuelled catch up, Purezza (North, no.50) has your back with their crusty, generously topped pizzas.

### Coffee (or tea) and cake

Enjoy a moreish peanut butter coffee and a big selection of sweet treats on the comfy sofas at WAVE (East, no.17). Or head to Brick Lane's Vida Bakery (East, no.9) for a slice of their signature six-layered rainbow cake and a pot of tea.

### Convincing non-vegan friends

Chow down on some dumplings, bao and spicy dan dan noodles with a beer or two at Mao Chow (East, no.29). If you fancy Indian, Spicebox's (East, no.35) chick'n korma and shroom keema will have the most die-hard meat eater converted to the joys of plant-based eating.

# KALIFORNIA KITCHEN

*Upbeat, colourful all-day diner*

VEGAN

Peering through the hot-pink frontage – or scrolling through the Instagram feed – of this flower-bedecked restaurant, it might appear as though Kalifornia Kitchen is all about looks. And, of course, the presentation is spot on with pink pickles and edible blooms adorning the plates. But as you dig in to jackfruit tacos or the pretzel bun burger and crispy fries, the delicate, moreish flavours tell a more layered tale. Your plates will empty fast, leaving you with a hunger for more.

*19 Percy Street, W1T 1DY*
*Nearest station: Goodge Street*
*Other location: Fulham*
*kaliforniakitchen.co.uk @kaliforniakitchen*

# TREDWELLS

*Elegant modern British dining*

VEGAN FRIENDLY

Cocktail shakers rattle and black-apron-clad waiters attentively swish past; the atmosphere in this white-tablecloth restaurant is as lively as the Soho scene outside, seen through the floor-to-ceiling windows. The vegan tasting menu highlights British seasonal produce with delicately prepared dishes like Jersey Royals with seaside succulents, pea tortellini and Yorkshire rhubarb. The non-vegan tasting menu may look a little more substantial but go with the excellent wine pairings and you'll soon forget any potential culinary inequities.

*4A Upper St Martin's Lane, WC2H 9NY*
*Nearest station: Leicester Square*
*tredwells.com @tredwells*

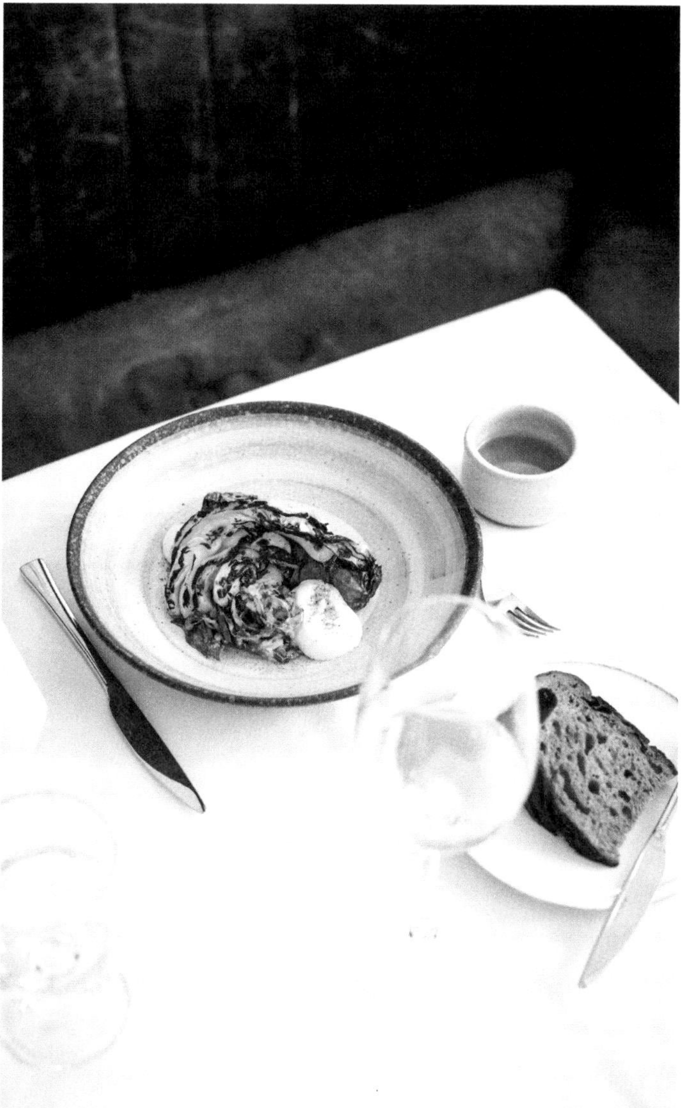

# CROSSTOWN

*Moreish doughnut and coffee shop*

VEGAN FRIENDLY

If you haven't already discovered this New York-inspired chain of carefully crafted sourdough doughnuts then you're in for a lemon-thymey, peanut-buttery glazed treat. The Marylebone branch is exclusively vegan but all Crosstown shops and stalls, from Canary Wharf to Broadway Market, carry an extensive vegan range. The minimal black-and-white shop interior brings the central glass cabinet into focus, where a glistening array of jewel-like treasures wait to be chosen (the hard bit) before being devoured (easy).

*5-6 Picton Place, W1U 1BL*
*Nearest station: Bond Street*
*Other locations: multiple, see website*
*crosstowndoughnuts.com*
*@crosstowndoughnuts*

# CHAI BY MIRA

*Ultra-comforting wellbeing café*

VEGAN FRIENDLY

Whether you've just stepped out of a vinyasa class or need a break from shopping on nearby Carnaby Street, this cosy café inside Triyoga studio will put a smile on your face. Yoga enthusiast Mira Manek, who has written two books – one about modern-day Ayurvedic rituals and another offering healthy takes on traditional Gujarati recipes – knows a thing or two about the therapeutic potential of food. Sip a fragrant rose chai, nibble on a slice of saffron key lime pie or fill up with a delightfully non-London priced soup or khichri (an Ayurvedic rice and pulse dish). Recharge complete.

*Triyoga Soho, 2nd Floor, Kingly Court, WIB 5PW*
*Nearest station: Oxford Circus*
*chaibymira.com  @chaibymira*

5

# PHO

*Fresh Vietnamese street food*

VEGAN FRIENDLY

When hunger hits hard in the busier parts
of town, this nationwide chain is there like
a reliable old friend. Vegan options are no
afterthought here – tofu did originate in Asia,
after all – and the huge bowls of steaming noodle
soup, piled high with fragrant herbs, arrive fast
and fresh. The cosy, lived-in interiors feel private
and relaxed, whether you're alone or in a group.
Grab your bowl and let the aroma of Thai basil
revive your senses and power you through
the rest of your day – or night.

*163-165 Wardour Street, W1F 8WN*
*Nearest station: Tottenham Court Road*
*Other locations: multiple, see website*
*phocafe.co.uk  @phorestaurant*

# 6

# ETHOS

*No-nonsense vegetarian buffet*

VEGAN FRIENDLY

Steps away from the madness of Oxford Street
lies this buffet restaurant heaving with fresh,
simple dishes. Paying by weight means you may for
the first time notice how heavy roast cauliflower,
sweetcorn fritters and lasagne can be – but this is
more than made up for by the smug feeling of
scoring some 'real food' among the chain stores
and tourist traps of the West End.

*48 Eastcastle Street, W1W 8DX*
*Nearest station: Oxford Circus*
*ethosfoods.com @ethosfoods*

7

# GENESIS

*Organic fast-food diner*

VEGAN

Step through to another dimension, where hot
dogs, cheese sticks and superfood cocktails are
organic, photogenic and bathed in pink neon light.
While Genesis manages to pull off a kitsch
comic-book interior that many places could only
dream of, their wholesome approach to ingredients
(including avocado oil for deep frying) and the
world- and street-food-inspired menu guarantee
that this place is about far more than good looks.
Go for their classic 'dirty' dishes and make sure
you finish with a milkshake or soft serve –
one of the best in town.

144 Commercial Street, E1 6NU
*Nearest station: Shoreditch High Street*
*eatgenesis.com  @eatgenesis*

# 8

# BIFF'S JACK SHACK

*Jackfruit-based junk food*

VEGAN

For when nothing but the crispiest, deepest-fried junk – smothered with BBQ sauce or maple chipotle and stuck between buns – will do, Biff's has your back. In the Shoreditch branch in Boxpark you can catch a flicker of Bruce Lee on the vintage TV monitors while counting the seconds for your jackfruit burger and 'gnarly seitan bacun'-topped fries to arrive. Don't forget to add one of the four varieties of jackfruit wings – and don't panic if you find a piece of sugarcane 'bone' in there.

*Boxpark Shoreditch, 2-10 Bethnal Green Road, E1 6GY*
*Nearest station: Shoreditch High Street*
*Other locations: Walthamstow, Homerton*
*biffsjackshack.com @biffsjackshack*

# 9

# VIDA BAKERY

*Spell-binding gluten-free bakery*

VEGAN

You may not have realised it, but your life could well have a half-foot-high, rainbow-layered, cake-shaped hole in it right now. Luckily you can fill it fast, down on Brick Lane. Invite your best friend or your on-trend mother, and whisk them to this pastel-coloured haven for all things sweet, vegan and gluten-free. Next, each choose a hot drink, served in cute mismatched mugs, and succumb to the sugar-induced euphoria. Not someone with a huge sweet tooth? Go for a cupcake, with its perfect ratio of icing to cake.

*139 Brick Lane, E1 6SB*
*Nearest station: Shoreditch High Street*
*vidabakery.co.uk  @vidabakery*

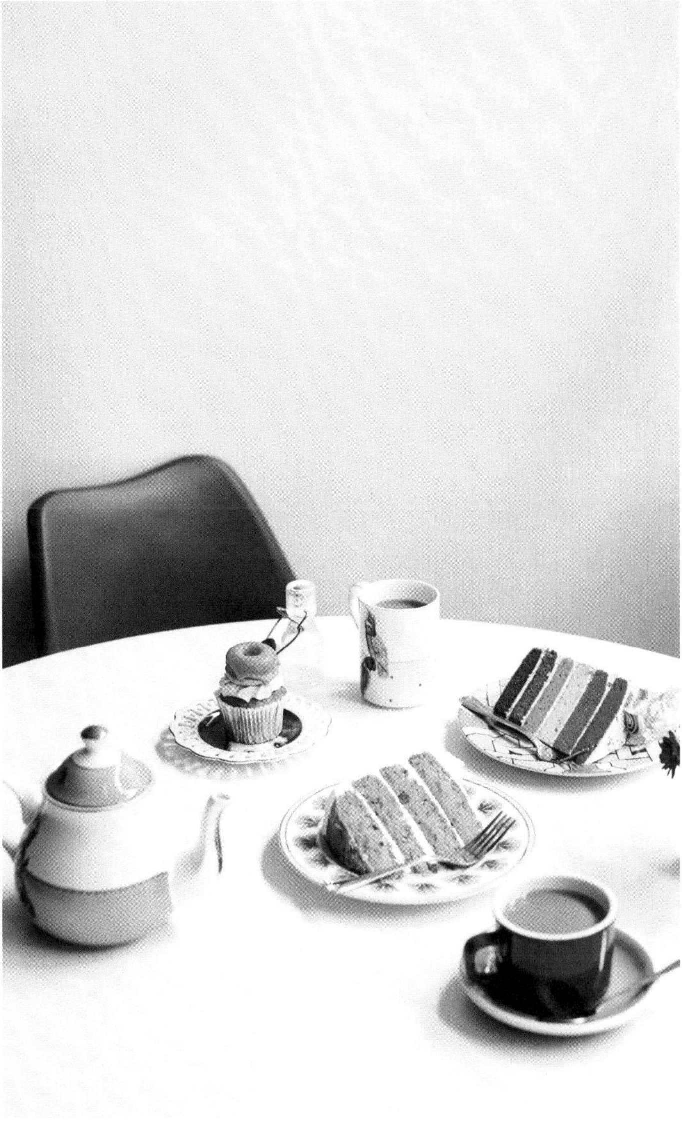

# 10

# MOTHER

*Canalside café, juice bar and takeaway*

VEGAN

Stroll past the busier, hipper end of Hackney Wick and you'll find Mother in what used to be part of the Olympics media hub. Lovingly conceived by three siblings, this is the local spot to gather at communal wooden tables for nourishing all-day breakfasts, fully loaded salad bowls and smoothies. Summers see the lively front area opened up to the River Lea, where locals linger over their smashed avo toast and acai bowls while watching canal boats glide past.

*Unit 1, Canalside, Here East Estate, E20 3BS*
*Nearest station: Hackney Wick*
*mother.works  @mother.works*

# 11

# THE VURGER CO.

*Burgers and shakes, deftly presented*

VEGAN

Napkins at the ready – you'll need them when
tucking into a jaw-dislocatingly tall Vurger,
along with skin-on fries and a chocolate hazelnut
milkshake. The stars of the show here are the
patties, made from beans and veggies rather than
meat-replacers, doused in a range of condiments:
spicy queso sauce, house mayo and all the crunchy,
pickled bits. Both branches give you the option
to buckle down with your burger al fresco – in
an outdoor seating area at the Hoxton branch,
or a quick escalator ride up to Jubilee Park
in Canary Wharf.

*6 Richmix Square, Cygnet Street, E1 6LD*
*Nearest station: Shoreditch High Street*
*Other location: Canary Wharf*
*thevurgerco.com  @thevurgerco*

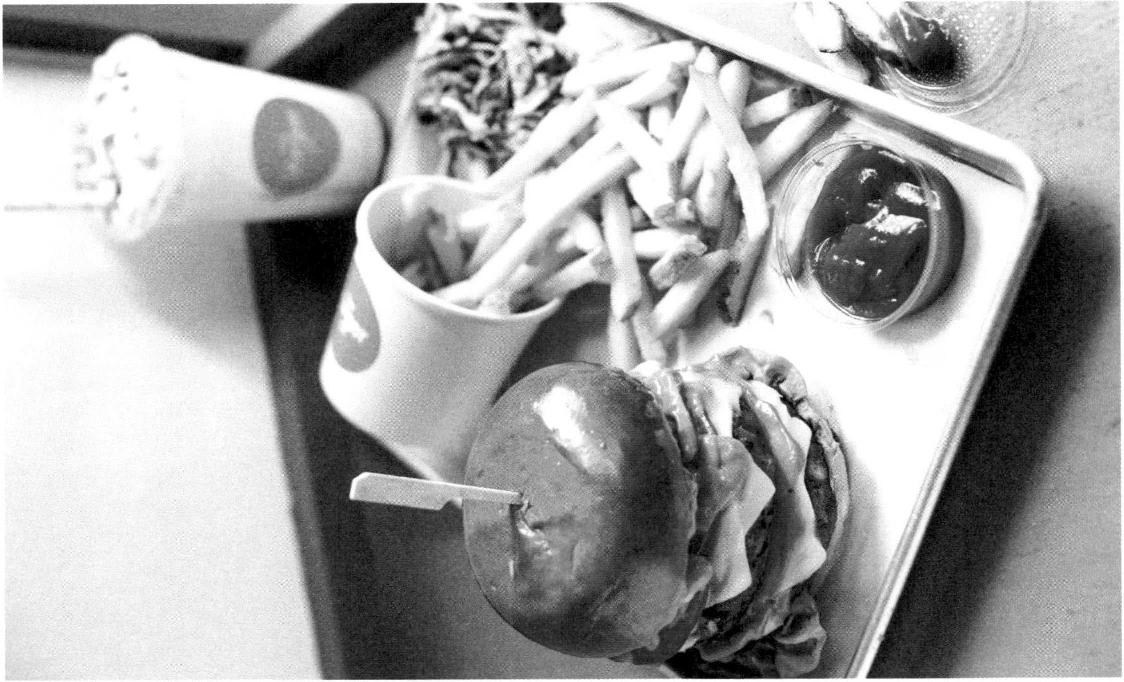

12

# LELE'S

*Relaxed neighbourhood café*

VEGAN

Imagine a friendly neighbour who invites you into their floral-patterned living room, pours you a strong coffee, then cooks you a plateful of the best French toast scattered with edible blooms. It may sound like a dream, but if you find yourself in this corner of Hackney, head to Lele's to get your fill of delicately executed café classics – avo or mushrooms on toast, weekend 'hangover fixes' and an ever-shifting range of cakes and buns baked in-house. Four-legged friends will be delighted to find their own jar of biscuits among the potted plants and mismatched vintage furniture.

*50 Lower Clapton Road, E5 0RN*
*Nearest station: Hackney Central*
*leleslondon.com @leles_london*

13

# AUN

*Japanese-fusion restaurant*

VEGAN FRIENDLY

A perfect little slice of Japan awaits you on Stoke Newington Church Street: a new-generation eatery the likes of which you might find in a hip Osaka neighbourhood. The colours are muted, the menu down-to-earth yet inventive, with cross-cultural dishes like mushroom ajillo or sun-dried tomato and shiso nori rolls offering a fresh take on Japanese food. Sample their vegan tasting menu and wash it down with sake (cold, not hot) from hand-made, wabi-sabi-wonky, ceramic cups.

*178 Stoke Newington Church Street, N16 0JL*
*Nearest station: Stoke Newington*
*aun-restaurant.com  @aunstokenewington*

# 14

# I WILL KILL AGAIN
# & DARK ARTS COFFEE

*Craft coffee and comfort food*

VEGAN FRIENDLY

As the name of this café's in-house coffee roastery suggests, some deliciously dark art is being practised in this formerly derelict building just off Homerton High Street. As coffees are stirred and magick cast over the spiced seitan-chorizo stews and the adobo lemon cream and buckwheat waffles, you'll soon fall under the spell: the mix of innovative comfort food and black humour is an irresistible, and refreshing, combination. When you've had your fill, order a homemade vegan brownie for the road – you'll be glad you did.

*1-5 Rosina Street, E9 6JH*
*Nearest station: Homerton*
*darkartscoffee.co.uk  @iwillkillagain*

# LA FAUXMAGERIE

*Artisan cheese shop*

VEGAN

You'll easily spot what looks like a stylish,
traditional cheesemonger along Shoreditch's
Cheshire Street. On a closer look (and sniff) you'll
find ripened cashew camembert, smoky soy cheese
and cultured cashew cheddar lining the counter.
If you are new to the fledgling world of artisan
plant-based cheese, let the apron-clad experts guide
you through the many UK-made offerings for sale.
You might discover a new secret weapon for
your next social gathering's cheeseboard.

*20 Cheshire Street, E2 6EH*
*Nearest station: Shoreditch High Street*
*lafauxmagerie.com  @lafauxmagerie*

EAST

# 16

# ESSENTIAL VEGAN

*Brazilian-inspired café*

VEGAN

Catch your breath and relax in this light-filled,
mellow space, where about half of the floor is
occupied by a homely open kitchen and the aroma
of freshly baked cakes waft through the air.
The menu salutes the founder's Latin roots, with
generous helpings of veganised Brazilian street
food joining classic but inventively spiced seitan
or jackfruit burgers and chips. Make sure to arrive
early if you want to catch one of the lunch specials
(these often sell out) – and don't dream of leaving
without trying the insanely addictive cheese balls.

*6 Calvert Avenue, E2 7JP*
*Nearest station: Shoreditch High Street*
*essentialvegan.uk  @essentialvegan*

# 17

# WAVE

*Imaginative dishes in a peaceful space*

VEGAN

Follow the WAVE sign on Mare Street and
bob down the alley to this plant-adorned space.
In warm weather you can sit out in the courtyard;
otherwise, sink into one of the sofas or have a go on
a hanging chair. Next, order a peanut butter coffee
(you read that right – and yes, it's unbelievably
moreish) and get choosing. Perhaps a banana
Biscoff freakshake? Or a stack of syrupy coconut-
bacun pancakes? If you prefer your treats savoury,
the sourdough toasts piled with toppings of garlic
mushrooms, seedy smashed avo or turmeric
tofu scramble will do nicely.

*11 Dispensary Lane, E8 1FT*
*Nearest station: Hackney Central*
*wearevegaNeverything.com*
*@we_are_vegan_everything*

# 18

# THE BRIGHT STORE

*Café, shop and community hub*

VEGAN

Come visit the home of ethical lifestyle
magazine *Bright*: a café and store with a members'
club in the basement. The compact space echoes
the clean black-and-white layout of the magazine,
and gathers some of the capital's most active and
innovative movers and shakers, makers and bakers
under one roof, both as suppliers and patrons.
Pop in for a coffee and croissant, strike up
conversation with like-minded strangers
and maybe even bag yourself a Vegan
Queen t-shirt while you're here.

*268 Hackney Road, E2 7SJ*
*Nearest station: Hoxton*
*brightzine.co/the-bright-store*
*@thebrightstoreldn*

19

# BLACK CAT

*No-fuss hearty meals*

VEGAN

Anyone who's been vegan or veggie for a while
will enjoy a sense of nostalgia at this workers'
cooperative just off Mare Street. Curry, pies and
lasagne are served up in generous portions and
taste fresh, home-cooked and reminiscent of many
happy summers spent at festivals. The library
of activist titles, posters and evening events hint at
the café's anarchist spirit, while the unpretentious
decor and communal tables guarantee that
everyone feels welcome.

*76A Clarence Road, E5 8HB*
*Nearest station: Hackney Downs*
*blackcatcafe.co.uk  @blackcathackney*

# 20

# CUB

*Modern fine dining, without the stuffiness*
VEGAN FRIENDLY

The moment you step into this intimate, sophisticated
space, with its saffron-yellow upholstered booths
(and, look closely, table tops made out of recycled
yogurt cups), you know you're in for something special.
With impeccable sustainability credentials and
attention to flavour that borders on the obsessive,
the set menu transforms ingredients gathered from
small British producers – seaweeds, hay-smoked roots,
microorganisms and rare blooms – into a playful
sequence of edible delight. The cocktails are as
fabulous as the food – and that stalk of pok choi main?
It may just be the best green leaf you've ever tasted.

*153 Hoxton Street, N1 6PJ*
*Nearest station: Hoxton*
*lyancub.com  @lyan.cub*

# 21

# ANDU CAFÉ

*Ethiopian BYOB café*

VEGAN

Some places become part of your routine for simple
reasons – at this humble café, the combination
of tasty, affordable food, great location and
the option to bring your own drinks to kick off
a night out, goes a long way. Fading 90s Ethiopian
travel posters and knick-knacks cover the walls
and the menu has pretty much just one offering,
the sampler platter, made to perfection. Fuel up
on the berbere lentil stew and other delicately
spiced vegetable dishes, all mopped up with
squidgy injera bread, before heading on to
one of the many nightspots nearby.

*528 Kingsland Road, E8 4AH*
*Nearest station: Dalston Junction*
*anducafe.co.uk*

# 22

# HOUSE OF VEGAN

*Weekend street-food market*

VEGAN

The iconic Truman Brewery's Boiler House
(the one with the imposing chimney) has for years
been a pitstop for Brick Lane weekend loafers on
the hunt for food and beer. Boldly, in late 2018 it
went completely vegan. From junk to ethnic, healthy
to sweet, the dishes sold from the stalls crowding
the floor will satisfy any craving. Add a well-stocked
bar, a DJ and a mezzanine eating area, metal beams
and exposed brick walls, and the warehouse vibe is
complete. Vintage shopping, people watching and
sampling some of London's tastiest street food –
that's your Shoreditch Sunday sorted.

*The Boiler House, 152 Brick Lane, E1 6RU*
*Nearest station: Shoreditch High Street*
*@houseofveganldn*

# 23

# LOVE SHACK

*Paradise island hangout, backpacker style*

VEGAN

Blink and you might miss the small settlement beside the old railway arches right by Cambridge Heath station. But look closer: this former wasteland has been revived by three old school friends into a light-festooned, makeshift getaway complete with beach bar, deckchairs and hammocks – you won't even notice you're next to the A107. You may as well put your backpack down and stay for the next few days, grazing on the menu of smoothies, rustic fried breakfasts and burgers with loaded fries, catching a gig (check their social media for listings), or sipping 'hot-tails' in winter.

*Arch 298, 299 Cambridge Heath Road, E2 9HA*
*Nearest station: Cambridge Heath*
*loveshackldn.com @loveshack_ldn*

# 24

# HORNBEAM CAFÉ

*Delicious, non-profit community café*

VEGAN

Even if you're not a Walthamstow local, this café is one to watch. Many vegan food talents cut their teeth in residencies here: Spicebox (no.35) and Palm Greens (no.25), for example. Volunteer-built as an environmentalists' centre in 1994, Hornbeam is deep-rooted in the local community and hosts a wide range of events, from herbal medicine workshops to Afro-Brazilian drumming for kids. When there is no residency, volunteers prepare pay-as-you-feel meals using locally sourced ingredients that would otherwise go to waste. Keep an eye on their social media feeds to find out who the next food star will be.

*458 Hoe Street, E17 9AH*
*Nearest station: Walthamstow Central*
*hornbeam.org.uk  @hornbeam_cafe*

25

# PALM GREENS

*Nourishing lunchtime salads*

VEGAN

London Fields may be rife with vegan offerings, but few of them give you a rooftop view with your California-inspired kale Caesar or freekeh-mint-cauli salad. Climb the stairs up to NT's bar, located in Netil House studio space, where you can enjoy Palm Greens' fresh, international flavours on the massive terrace (in good weather) or indoors, where comfy sofas offer the same fabulous view. This fern-adorned hideaway shifts into a buzzing bar and gig venue at night, but be aware that the post-4pm food offerings aren't vegan.

*NT's, Netil House, 1 Westgate Street, E8 3RL*
*Nearest station: London Fields*
*palmgreens.co.uk  @palmgreens*

# 26

# MILDREDS

*International menu in a smart setting*

VEGAN FRIENDLY

Mildreds is the reliable big sister of the London veggie scene, having served up a world-food-inspired menu from their original Soho location for over 30 years. Today there are three more branches scattered across London, with Dalston being the most spacious. Food choices are vegan-heavy and up-to-the-minute: if burgers are your thing, the buffalo chick'n burger with chipotle ketchup is a must. Otherwise, try some starters to share: dashi dumplings, Roman-style artichokes, pea and shallot ravioli. You may not be in for a culinary epiphany but, being the exemplary older sibling that she is, Mildreds can be counted on to deliver consistently grown-up food.

*1 Dalston Square, E8 3GU*
*Nearest station: Dalston Junction*
*Other locations: King's Cross, Soho, Camden*
*mildreds.co.uk  @mildredsrestaurants*

# 27

# COOKDAILY

*Soul-satisfying urban street food*

VEGAN

You might question your cool credentials when
entering this railway arch or wonder if you've
arrived at an all-day nightclub by mistake, but
you'll soon feel part of the crew – everyone is
welcome, everyone is here. Check the wall-mounted
menu for your pick of the day: Jungle Curry,
High Grade stir-fry (made with hemp oil),
Jerk Chick'n and Coco Soup all come served
in paper bowls over noodles or brown rice.
Then camp on the faux grass outside, or grab
a t-shirt-covered pouffe. It's no-frills
but it hits the spot.

*Arch 358, Westgate Street, E8 3RN*
*Nearest station: London Fields*
*cookdaily.co.uk  @cookdailylondon*

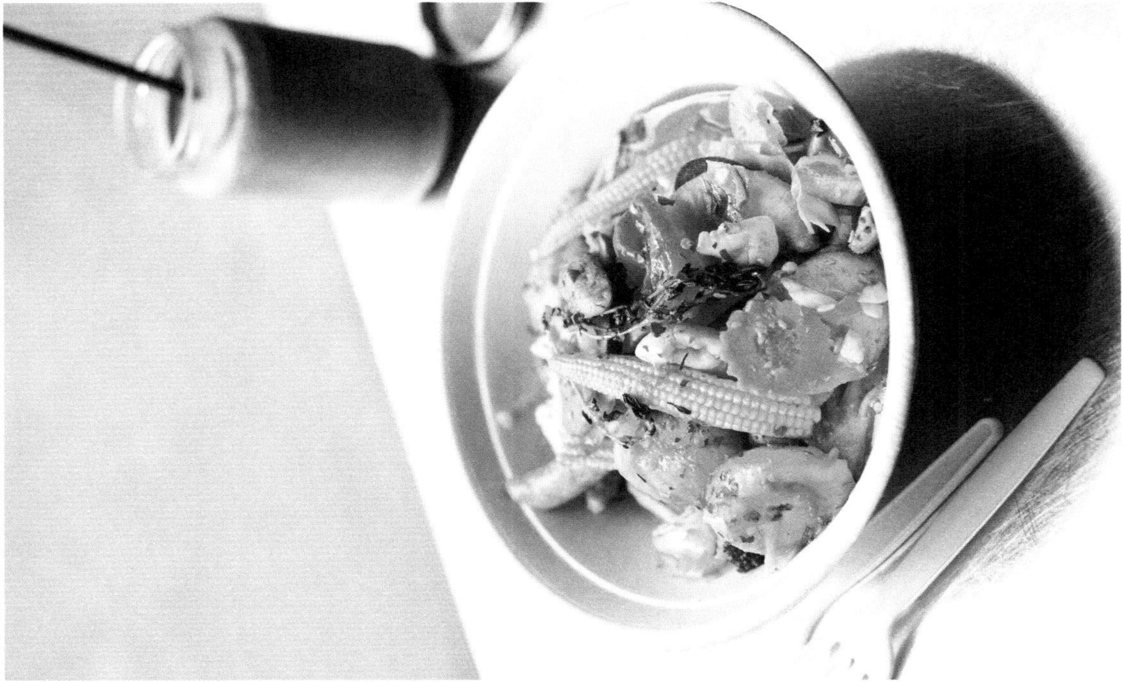

# 28

# 10 CABLE STREET

*Supperclubs and workshops in an arty home*

VEGAN

Ring the bell of the warm-grey wooden door of
10 Cable Street and the delightful owner Moko Sellars
will invite you in. Having spotted a lack of vegan-
friendly social places after turning vegan herself
in 2016, Moko decided to open up the ground floor
of her own home and invite some of London's most
creative entrepreneurs to co-host events she herself
would like to attend. Today the cheese and wine nights
are a hit, as are the workshops (bento masterclasses,
tofu-making and many more) and supperclubs covering
everything from Chinese hot pot to fine dining.
Always good times at 10 Cable Street.

*10 Cable Street, E1 8JG*
*Nearest station: Aldgate East*
*tencablestreet.com  @tencablestreet*

29

# MAO CHOW

*Innovative Chinese small plates*

VEGAN

This one-chef, one-waitress hole-in-the-wall will rock your world and possibly blow your mind if the 'Chinese moonshine' is on the menu. Sit yourself at the bright yellow table (there's just one, so prepare to make new friends), order everything, and get ready for an onslaught of bold and layered Sichuan-pepper-fuelled flavours. Umami-rich dan dan noodles, crispy oyster mushroom bao, the chef's secret blend of 'meaty veg', and the sticky Chinese doughnuts, will have you scrambling to visit again. Bring your non-vegan foodie friends that need wowing.

*159A Mare Street, E8 3RH*
*Nearest station: London Fields*
*mao-chow.com  @mao_chow*

# 30

# REDEMPTION

*Alcohol-free cocktails and comfort food*

VEGAN

This small group of restaurant-bars is there to support you in your quest for fun (without the alcohol), nourishing food (without the gluten) and the odd indulgent treat (without the refined sugar, obviously). With an impressive alcohol-free selection – high-end sparkling wine and innovative cocktails – and a touch of velvety glam, these are easy places for a date night or a catch-up, fuelled by jackfruit blue corn tacos, kimchi super slaw, and perhaps a kombucha apple mockjito.

*320 Old Street, EC1V 9DR*
*Nearest station: Old Street*
*Other locations: Notting Hill, Covent Garden*
*redemptionbar.co.uk  @redemptionbar*

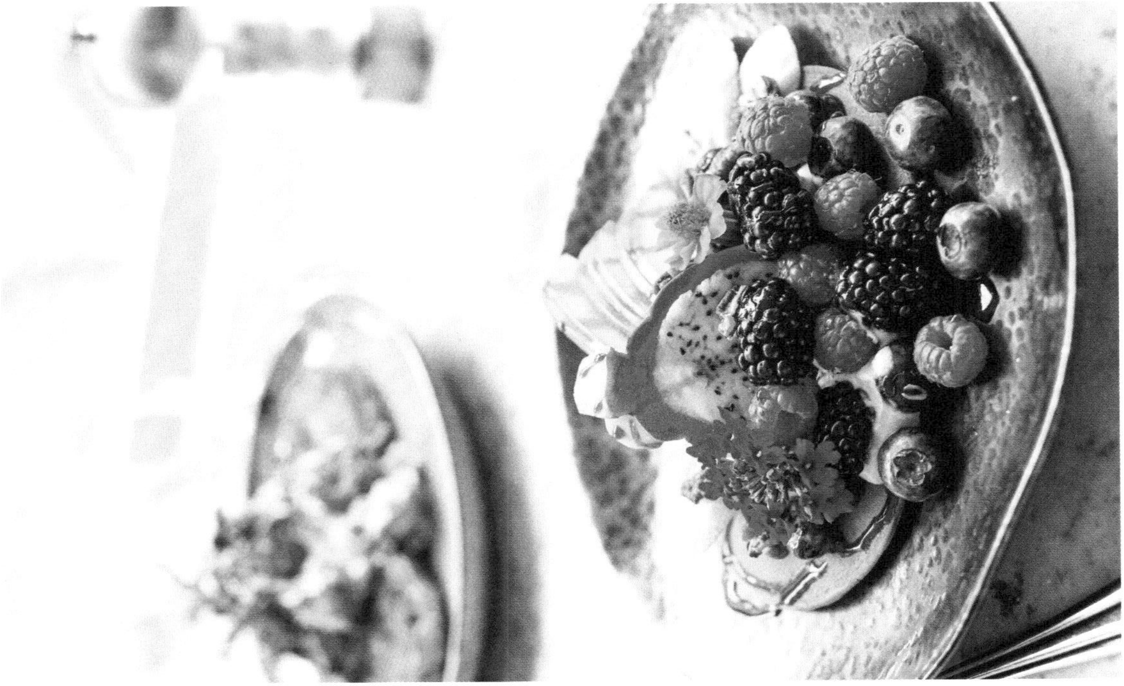

# 31

# PLANT HUB & ACADEMY

*Restaurant, bakery and cookery school*

VEGAN

What do you get when you take a chef, a cookbook
author and restaurateur, and a culinary school
instructor and drop them near London Fields?
An organic restaurant, gluten-free bakery and
cooking academy, of course. Pulling together
different strands of the more health-conscious, raw
end of the food spectrum, Plant Hub serves classics
with a spin. Try the gluten-free focaccia topped with
truffle mushroom and kale, the chickpea omelette
or aubergine parmigiana, and finish with a flower-
adorned gluten-free pea brownie. Inspired? Sign up
for a masterclass in anything from food styling
to molecular gastronomy.

*217 Mare Street, E8 3QE*
*Nearest station: London Fields*
*planthub.net  @planthubuk*
*@plantacademyuk*

# 32

# UNITY DINER

*Non-profit restaurant serving tasty classics*

VEGAN

Brainchild of vegan campaigner and social media star Ed Winters, this is the place to head if you want to eat in a prime east London location while also funding a good cause (all profits go to the animal rights organisation Surge and towards funding a new rescue sanctuary). Take your pick from the crowd-pleasing menu – burgers, tofish and chips, mac 'n' cheese and fully loaded salads – and join the lively conversations under the 'The Future is Vegan' neon sign.

*5 Hoxton Market, N1 6HG*
*Nearest station: Old Street*
*unitydiner.co.uk  @unitydiner*

# 33

# PILPEL

*Fresh, authentic, quality falafels*

VEGAN FRIENDLY

Sometimes all you want is perfect, simple falafel – crispy and hot, with creamy hummus and crunchy, tangy veg. But, as most people know, this deceptively straightforward dish can easily go wrong (yes, microwave oven, we're looking at you). If you're hit by a craving near a Pilpel branch – they're dotted around east London and the City – then join the fast-moving queue to enjoy the founder's homage to his grandad's Tel Aviv falafel stand. These falafels are spot on: authentic, delicious and served with a smile. The old man would definitely approve.

*60 Alie Street, E1 8PX*
*Nearest station: Aldgate East*
*Other locations: multiple, see website*
*pilpel.co.uk  @pilpelforthepeople*

# 34

# SMASHING KITCHEN

*Honest food in a welcoming space*

VEGAN

If you've ever had the kind of warm-hearted friend
who thrives on cooking hearty, healthy meals for
their loved ones, you'll feel right at home in this
little place just off Mare Street. Pop into the
light- and plant-filled space for your five-a-day,
served with a smile by the friendly manageress.
Try building your own salad bowl – either to eat
in our take out – and pile it high with veggies,
roast potatoes, buckwheat salad, guacamole and
cheesy butterbean hummus, all made from scratch
on the day. Unpretentious, and refreshingly
affordable for the area.

*1A Bayford Street, E8 3SE*
*Nearest station: London Fields*
*smashingkitchen.co.uk*
*@smashingkitchen*

# 35

# SPICEBOX

*New-generation curry house*

VEGAN

Wind down Walthamstow's Hoe Street to find this modern spin on the British curry house: street snacks, jalfrezi and chick'n korma, but not as you know them. Flavours are layered and natural, with crunchy, fresh textures exploding in your mouth – if only all Indian food could be like this. Come at night and the psychedelic, branded graphics and vibrant colour-blocked dining room may have you feeling like you've stumbled into a Varanasi alleyway after a particularly strong bhang lassi. Bring on the banana chai doffle.

*58 Hoe Street, E17 4PG*
*Nearest station: Walthamstow*
*eatspicebox.co.uk  @eatspicebox*

# 36

# VEGAN NIGHTS

*Monthly food rave*

VEGAN

It's a weeknight in the heart of Brick Lane and some of London's finest up-and-coming food vendors and DJs are gathered among a diverse, lively crowd of thousands – hungry for good food and a good party. From pizza to bánh mì, soft serve to churros – every type of street food is represented and there are market stalls to browse, too. This fast-evolving, festival-like event sees the vegan-curious and the long-converted rubbing shoulders, all clutching beers and boxes of food while throwing shapes on the dance floor. Just make sure to book online, in advance if you can.

*150 Brick Lane, E1 6QL*
*Nearest station: Shoreditch High Street*
*vegannights.uk  @vegannightsldn*

# 37

# THE SPREAD EAGLE

*London's first vegan pub*

VEGAN

If you find yourself pub-fatigued, head over to The Spread Eagle. Your faith in ordering nachos and fish burgers from a pub menu might bounce back too – in fact, any of the dishes, created by resident street-food stars Club Mexicana, will bring you joy. Neither a gastropub nor posh, the place offers a fresh take on pub culture: innovative drinks, happy staff and the chance to catch up with friends without losing your voice. The sexy sapphire blue interior and Prince shrine seal the deal.

*224 Homerton High Street, E9 6AS*
*Nearest station: Homerton*
*thespreadeaglelondon.co.uk*
*@thespreadeaglelondon*

# 38

# HETU

*Package-free, zero-waste shop*

VEGAN

When her career in finance stopped making
sense, Laura Boyes decided it was time to bring
the Australian concept of a zero-waste store to
her native London. Thus Hetu, meaning 'purpose'
in Sanskrit, was born. Today her peaceful shop
feels like an outpost among the Land Rover-lined
streets of Clapham, though it's not far from another
zero-waste outlet, The Source Bulk Foods. Bring
your own containers and fill up on the carefully
chosen, affordable fresh veg and wholefood
staples, including their delicious nut butter,
milled in-house.

*201 St John's Hill, SW11 1TH*
*Nearest station: Clapham Junction*
*hetu.co.uk  @hetu_uk*

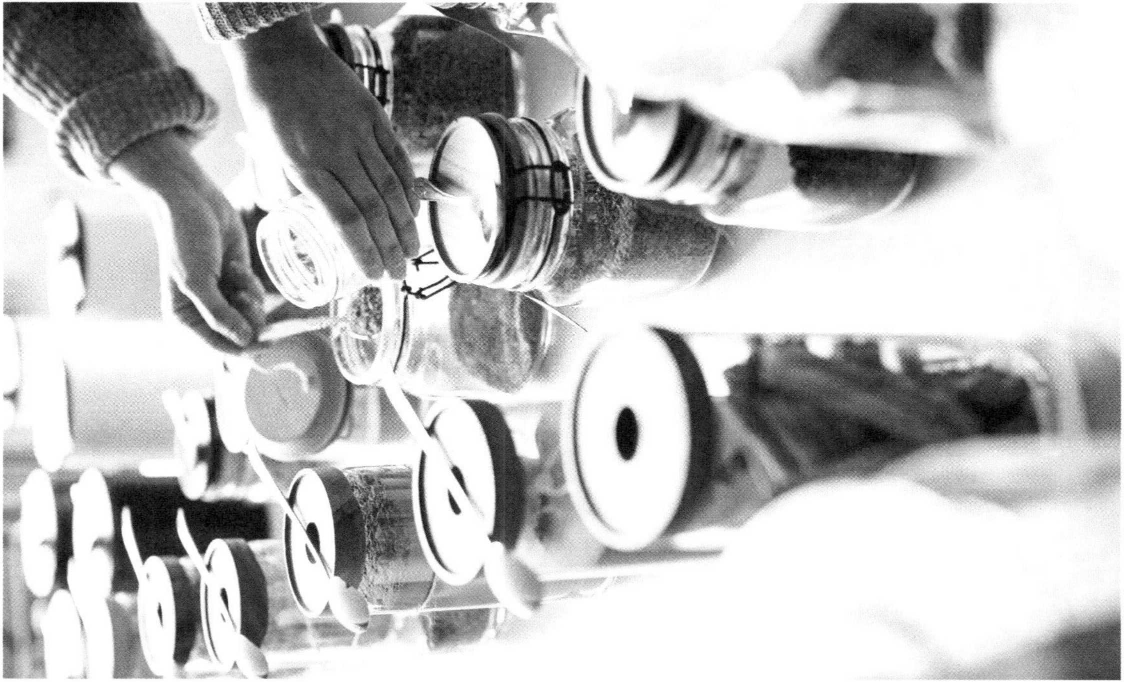

# 39

# CAFÉ VAN GOGH

*Friendly non-profit café*

VEGAN

A quirky iron sign at the leafy end of Brixton Road welcomes you to this community-run space. (And yes, Vincent van Gogh did live around the corner for a while.) Furniture that might have been thrifted from former trattorias and assembly halls, along with plants, books and paintings, create a whimsical backdrop for long conversations to be had over hearty ale pie and skin-on baked potato wedges. The café works with local charities to provide opportunities for young and vulnerable people, making every bite of their comfort classics taste even better. Don't miss the famous Sunday roast.

*88 Brixton Road, SW9 6BE*
*Nearest station: Oval*
*cafevangogh.co.uk  @cafevangogh01*

# 40

# PIPOCA VEGAN

*Crêperie and zero-waste shop*

VEGAN

Part café, part package-free shop, this cute spot is worth the detour from central Brixton. Long wooden shelves line the walls, packed with dispensers of every dry wholefood, oil and detergent you could possibly desire, while sacks of grains and giant tins of colourful preserves crowd the corners. The crêpes and brunch menu have a Latin-Caribbean twist, with homemade baked pinto beans, croquettes, Cajun spice and cassava chips joining classic favourites such as tofu scramble and sausages. Grab yourself a coffee and a snack at one of the tables before a spot of plastic-free shopping.

*224 Brixton Road, SW9 6AH*
*Nearest station: Brixton*
*facebook.com/pipocavegan*
*@pipocavegan*

# 41

# KIN + DEUM

*Modern Thai cooking*

VEGAN FRIENDLY

At the point just before London Bridge turns into buzzing Bermondsey, you may spot what looks like a cosily lit, tidy living room. Feel free to enter and join a lovely family affair where a sister-brother team of second-generation Thai restaurateurs merge traditional recipes with their young and savvy take on Bangkok street food. Glass noodle spring rolls and grandma's shiitake mushrooms, fragrant tom kha and aromatic massaman curry – all the crowd-pleasing dishes and flavours are here, in a fresh-tasting, quietly brilliant form.

*2 Crucifix Lane, SE1 3JW*
*Nearest station: London Bridge*
*Other locations: King's Cross, Soho, Camden*
*kindeum.com  @kindeum*

# 42

# FARMACY

*Organic farm-to-table restaurant*

VEGAN

Earthy meets glamorous in this much-hyped
Notting Hill destination, a bright, wood-bedecked
space where hand-thrown pots and rattan sit
alongside designer furniture and expensive hairstyles.
Living up to its name, Farmacy is all about the
health-promoting potential of plant-based food,
infusing a long, detailed menu with produce from
its own biodynamic Kentish farm. Everything from
the breakfast rawnola with housemade almond milk
to the mushroom-based Farmacy benedict – not
forgetting the CBD-infused mock- and cocktails
– tastes as good as it makes you feel.

*74-76 Westbourne Grove, W2 5SH*
*Nearest station: Bayswater*
*farmacylondon.com  @farmacyuk*

# 43

# EGERTON
# HOUSE HOTEL

*Posh afternoon tea with all the trimmings*

VEGAN FRIENDLY

Don your glad rags and head to luxury boutique
hotel Egerton House for a full-blown high tea
experience that's vegan (as long as you don't mind
the sight of pampered pups enjoying their 'doggy
afternoon tea' – not vegan). The window seats in the
restful, cream-coloured drawing room are the perfect
setting to pick at tiers of sandwiches, scones with
clotted coconut cream and delicate pastries, brought
to you by the impeccably attentive butler – with
a big pot of fine tea, of course. Book ahead
and treat your mum or best friend.

*17-19 Egerton Terrace, SW3 2BX*
*Nearest station: South Kensington*
*egertonhousehotel.com  @egerton_house*

# 44

# THE GATE

*World cuisine in a modern setting*

VEGAN FRIENDLY

In 1989, two young Iraqi-Indian-Jewish brothers
opened one of London's first vegetarian restaurants
in rented space in a community centre. And so,
The Gate Hammersmith was born. Three more
branches and many awards later, The Gate's
tried-and-tested global menu will suit most
occasions – whether you're eating with grandma,
business clients or a group of friends. Go for
the mezze sharing starter, follow with wild
mushroom risotto cake and save
some space for tiramisu.

*22-24 Seymour Place, W1H 7NL*
*Nearest station: Marble Arch*
*Other locations: Islington, Hammersmith, St John's Wood*
*thegaterestaurants.com @gaterestaurant*

# 45

# TELL YOUR FRIENDS

*Laidback spot for feel-good food*

VEGAN

Need a cosy west London destination for a date or a catch-up? This conservatory-fronted restaurant, brainchild of TV's *Made in Chelsea* star Lucy Watson, feels as calm and well-behaved as its verdant neighbourhood. Snag a seat on a cushion-scattered bench beneath the obligatory vegan-restaurant neon sign and opt for a selection of starters and sharers: whole, baked cashew camembert, cassava gyoza and chick'n bites – not made from seitan, refreshingly, but jackfruit chunks – are some of the most popular. Add a glass of rosé and a good conversation and you're all set.

*175 New King's Road, sw6 4sw*
*Nearest station: Parsons Green*
*tellyourfriendsldn.com  @tyfldn*

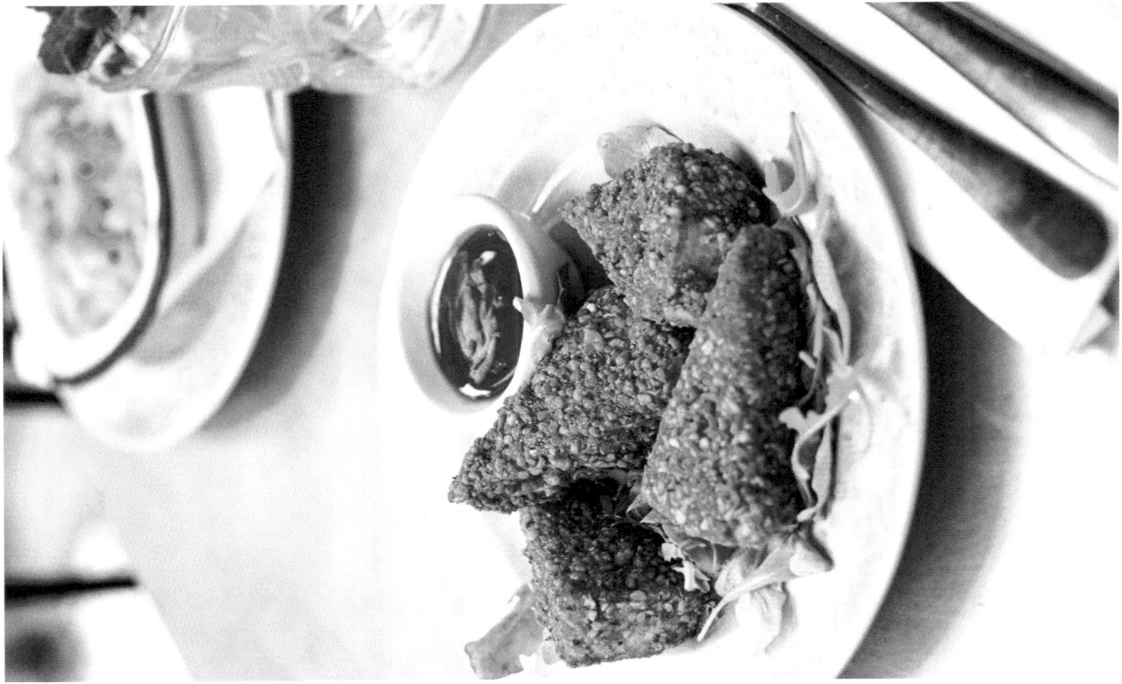

# 46

# RUDY'S DIRTY VEGAN DINER

*American-style fast food*

VEGAN

Bury your face in Rudy's famous Reuben sandwich – a stack of finely sliced seitan-pastrami within generously dressed rye bread – and be transported to a roadside diner somewhere along a Pennsylvania highway. In reality you may be dodging vloggers and sightseers in Camden Market, but Rudy's provides a hospitable pitstop with every friendly greeting and overflowing paper box. Come for the Reuben, stay for the Volcanic burger and don't forget the seasoned fries. It all makes for an indulgent doggy-bag snack back home, too.

*Unit 729-731, Camden Stables Market, NW1 8AH*
*Nearest station: Camden Town*
*@rudysdvd*

# 47

# NEM NEM

*Inventive Vietnamese cuisine*

VEGAN FRIENDLY

The interior may not have the cool factor
of some of the new kids on the vegan block,
but how many restaurants can show off an entire
vegan menu alongside their already extensive
traditional one? Imaginative dishes like vege fish
(seaweed-marinated aubergine) and betel-wrapped
tofu sit alongside Asian mock-meat pho and seitan
chick'n stir-fries. This is the perfect place to
deep-dive into the meat-free territories of
Vietnamese cuisine, rooted in traditional
Buddhist beliefs of non-violence.
Now if that's not cool…

*279 Upper Street, N1 2TZ*
*Nearest station: Highbury and Islington*
*nemnemrestaurant.co.uk  @nemnemrestaurant*

# 48

# THE FIELDS BENEATH

*Craft coffee and wholesome café food*

VEGAN

When the owner went vegan in 2017, so did his coffee shop. Since then, dairy-free lattes, bánh mì croissants and slabs of mum's banana bread have lifted this Kentish Town West railway arch to new heights. A daily fixture for many locals, The Fields Beneath has the lived-in feel of your best friend's kitchen – except here there are six different kinds of plant milk in the fridge, a traffic sign pointing to 'Vegans' and a trusty coffee machine that whirrs into action at 7am sharp. Kentish Town not on your route? Check out the Camden branch, which opened in 2019.

*52A Prince of Wales Road, NW5 3LN*
*Nearest station: Kentish Town West*
*Other location: Camden Town*
*thefieldsbeneath.com  @fieldsbeneath*

# 49

# CRAVING COFFEE
# & TOTTENHAM SOCIAL

*Artisan café hosting weekly pop-ups*

VEGAN FRIENDLY

Tottenham may not yet be on your culinary bucket list, but this outpost supplies the neighbourhood with its quota of oat flat whites and charcoal sourdough toast. Their weekly Tottenham Social nights invite different street-food traders into the kitchen – while these aren't always fully vegan, all vendors offer good vegan options. Fill up on everything from soul food seitan chick'n to Hong Kong curry 'fish' balls or Venezuelan pulled plantain arepa before heading down the road to Five Miles bar for a great choice of vegan craft beers on tap and a spot of late-night dancing.

*3 Gaunson House, Markfield Road, N15 4QQ*
*Nearest station: Seven Sisters*
*cravingcoffee.co.uk  @cravingcoffeeuk*

# 50

# PUREZZA

*Rustic, family-friendly sourdough pizzas*

VEGAN

Grab a few friends and cosy up in a
wood-panelled booth in what feels like
the contemporary offspring of a long lineage
of pizzerias. Hit the pizza end of the menu and,
regardless of dietary choices, everyone will be
delighted by the blistered sourdough crust loaded
with an up-to-date choice of toppings. Melty,
in-house-produced brown rice mozzarella with
roasted aubergines, wild forest mushrooms
or BBQ pieces all hit the spot.

*43 Parkway, NW1 7PN*
*Nearest station: Camden Town*
*purezza.co.uk  @purezza*

# 51

# CARAVAN

*Antipodean-inspired fusion dining*

VEGAN FRIENDLY

Caravan, with its industrial interior and chic
clientele, is all about effortless style. These
restaurants – five of them, at the last count, but each
with individual character – have a relaxed set-up,
with a long, creative and globally inspired menu.
The small plates and bowl dishes are strong on
plant-based options: from crispy chilli-salt tofu
to burnt sprouting broccoli with curry leaf oil. Try
the spacious and busy King's Cross branch for
dinner and drinks (they have a stellar cocktail list)
or the more intimate Exmouth Market location
for a midweek lunchtime catch-up.

*1 Granary Square, N1C 4AA*
*Nearest station: King's Cross St Pancras*
*Other locations: multiple, see website*
*caravanrestaurants.co.uk  @caravanrestaurants*

# 52

# WHAT THE PITTA

*Not-so-dirty kebab house*

VEGAN

Get ready for a superhero version of that
late-night guilty pleasure: the döner kebab.
In this clean, stainless-steel-shiny space just off
Camden High Street (with locations in Shoreditch
and Croydon Boxparks, too), you can marvel at the
uncanny familiarity of it all while knowing that the
only meat in your meal is perfectly spiced strips
of soy. Add crunchy salad, addictively creamy sauce
– and perhaps some onion rings on the side – and
you're all set. One regret? They stop serving before
11pm, which doesn't help when you're hit by
a 4am kebab craving after a great night out.

*89-91 Bayham Street, NW1 0AG*
*Nearest station: Camden Town*
*Other locations: Croydon, Shoreditch*
*whatthepitta.com @whatthepitta*

# 53

# WILD FOOD CAFÉ

*Photogenic, raw-centric dining*

VEGAN

Wild-at-heart city dwellers will be thrilled to find
this leafy space right on busy Upper Street. Here,
in the rose quartz and tourmaline hued interior, soft
tunes playing in the background, you can almost
imagine yourself in an enchanted forest. The drinks
list is laced with sophisticated superfoods – pine
pollen, lucuma, colloidal minerals – but it's
the desserts that bring the magic. Go for the raw
rainbow-layered cheesecake and a pistachio caramel
slice, and order a pot of cordyceps-enriched tea
to wash it all down.

*269-270 Upper Street, N1 2UQ*
*Nearest station: Highbury and Islington*
*Other location: Covent Garden*
*wildfoodcafe.com @wildfoodcafe_islington*

# INDEX

*(in alphabetical order)*

*An Opinionated Guide to Vegan London*

First edition

First published in 2019 by
Hoxton Mini Press, London
www.hoxtonminipress.com

Text by Sara Kiyo Popowa
All photography © Sam A. Harris
Copy-editing by Samantha Cook and Faith McAllister
Design and sequence by Daniele Roa
Production by Anna De Pascale

Compiled by Sara Kiyo Popowa and Hoxton Mini Press
With thanks to Matthew Young for initial series design

ISBN: 978-1-910566-56-5

A CIP catalogue record for this book is available from the British Library.

Printed and bound by OZGraf, Poland

MIX
Paper from
responsible sources
FSC® C002795
FSC
www.fsc.org